Incredible Dinosaur Facts

by Ruth Owen

Consultant:
Dougal Dixon, Paleontologist
Member of the Society of Vertebrate Paleontology
United Kingdom

BEARPORT
PUBLISHING

New York, New York

Credits

Cover, © Herschel Hoffmeyer/Shutterstock; 2–3, © Herschel Hoffmeyer/Shutterstock; 4, © Sanunyu L/Shutterstock; 4–5, © Linda Bucklin/Shutterstock; 6, © mohamad Haghani/Alamy; 7, © Michael Rosskothen/Shutterstock; 8T, © Herschel Hoffmeyer/Shutterstock; 8B, © Stocktrek Images, Inc./Alamy; 9, © National Geographic Image Collection/Alamy; 10, © ImageBroker/Alamy; 11, © Daniel Eskridge/Shutterstock; 12, © James Kuether; 13, © Creative Commons; 14, © Woudloper/Creative Commons; 15, © Herschel Hoffmeyer/Shutterstock; 16, © Greg Erickson; 17, © Herschel Hoffmeyer/Shutterstock; 18, © Catmando/Shutterstock; 19, © Herschel Hoffmeyer/Shutterstock and © Michael Rosskothen/Shutterstock; 20T, © Eva Maria Griebeler; 20BL, © michaeljung/Shutterstock; 20BR, © Elena Elenaphotos21/Alamy; 21T, © Steve Vidler/Alamy; 21B, © Fernandez et al/Public Domain; 22T, © Ondrej Prosicky/Shutterstock; 22B, © kikujungboy/Shutterstock; 23T, © Dotted Yeti/Shutterstock; 23B, © FrameStockFootages/Shutterstock.

Publisher: Kenn Goin
Senior Editor: Joyce Tavolacci
Creative Director: Spencer Brinker
Image Researcher: Ruth Owen Books

Library of Congress Cataloging-in-Publication Data

Names: Owen, Ruth, 1967– author.
Title: Incredible dinosaur facts / by Ruth Owen.
Description: New York, New York : Bearport Publishing, [2019] | Series: The dino-sphere | Includes bibliographical references and index.
Identifiers: LCCN 2018049819 (print) | LCCN 2018053170 (ebook) | ISBN 9781642802559 (ebook) | ISBN 9781642801866 (library)
Subjects: LCSH: Dinosaurs—Juvenile literature.
Classification: LCC QE861.5 (ebook) | LCC QE861.5 .O8459 2019 (print) | DDC 567.9—dc23
LC record available at https://lccn.loc.gov/2018049819

For more information, write to Bearport Publishing Company, Inc., 45 West 21st Street, Suite 3B, New York, New York 10010. Printed in the United States of America.

10 9 8 7 6 5 4 3 2 1

Contents

Amazing Dinosaurs 4

Biggest and Smallest 6

The Most Horns 8

A Musical Dinosaur 10

Hard-Headed! 12

The Longest Claws 14

Most Powerful Bite 16

Brain Size Matters 18

Dinosaur Eggs 20

Glossary 22

Index 24

Read More 24

Learn More Online 24

About the Author 24

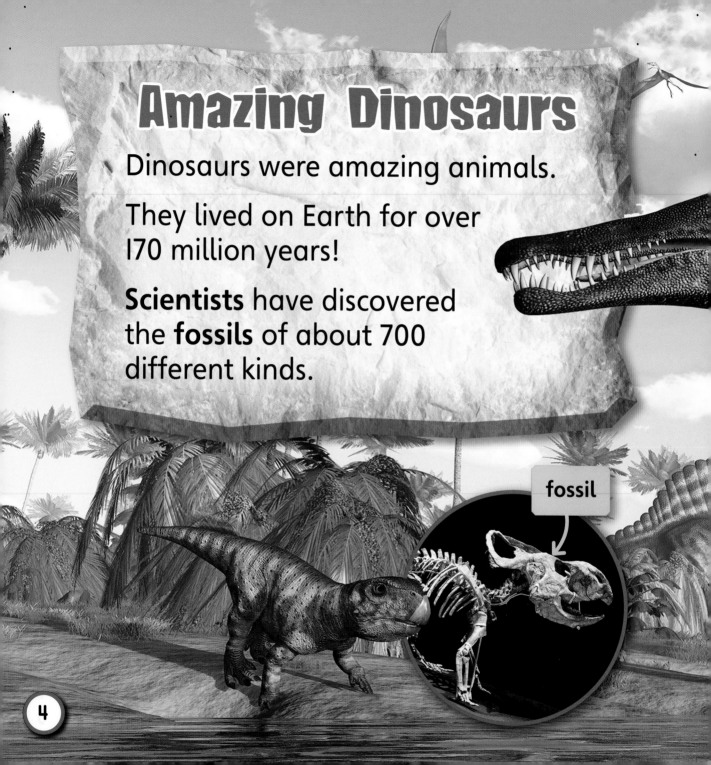

Amazing Dinosaurs

Dinosaurs were amazing animals.

They lived on Earth for over 170 million years!

Scientists have discovered the **fossils** of about 700 different kinds.

fossil

The word *dinosaur* comes from Greek words meaning "terrible lizard."

Spinosaurus
(spine-oh-SAWR-uhs)

5

Biggest and Smallest

Patagotitan was one of the biggest dinosaurs!

It was as tall as a five-story building.

It stretched the length of four school buses.

Patagotitan
(pa-tah-GO-tye-tuhn)

One of the smallest dinosaurs was *Microraptor*.

It had four wings and was tinier than a chicken.

Microraptor
(MYE-crow-rap-tuhr)

Argentinosaurus
(ar-JEN-tee-noh-sawr-uhs)

Argentinosaurus was one of the heaviest dinosaurs. It may have weighed as much as 18 elephants!

The Most Horns

A dinosaur called *Triceratops* had 3 horns—but *Kosmoceratops* had 15!

Triceratops (trye-SER-uh-tops)

Kosmoceratops (cos-mo-SER-uh-tops)

Kosmoceratops had two long horns on top of its head.

It had three short horns on its face.

It also had ten spikes behind its skull.

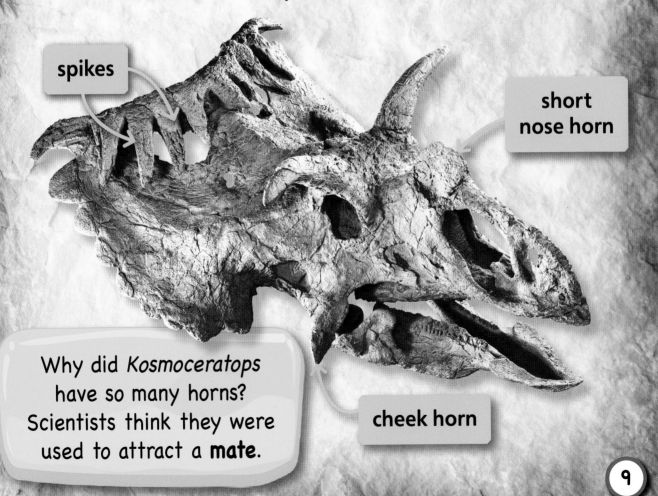

spikes

short nose horn

Why did *Kosmoceratops* have so many horns? Scientists think they were used to attract a **mate**.

cheek horn

A Musical Dinosaur

Parasaurolophus had a long **crest** on its head.

The crest had hollow tubes inside.

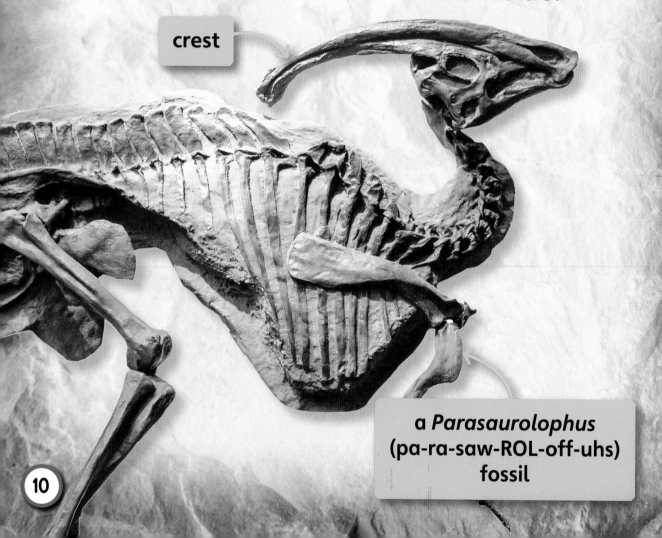

crest

a *Parasaurolophus*
(pa-ra-saw-ROL-off-uhs)
fossil

Some scientists think this dinosaur could blow air into the tubes.

This might have made a loud, booming noise—like an organ!

The crest could grow up to 6 feet (1.8 m) long.

Hard-Headed!

Get ready. Get set. *Crash!*

Pachycephalosaurus
(PAK-ee-seff-ah-loh-sawr-uhs)

Pachycephalosaurus
was a dinosaur with
a built-in helmet.

Its skull was up to 10 inches (25 cm) thick.
Scientists think this dinosaur used its head as a battering ram!

cracked skull

bony lumps and spikes

Scientists have found cracked fossil skulls. This shows that the dinosaurs butted heads.

The Longest Claws

A dinosaur called *Therizinosaurus* had super long claws!

Did the dinosaur use its claws to hunt?

claws

Amazingly, scientists think *Therizinosaurus* ate plants.

Therizinosaurus
(THUR-rit-zee-no-sawr-us)

The claws could grow up to 3 feet (0.9 m) long.

Most Powerful Bite

Which dinosaur had the most powerful jaws?

To find out, a scientist measured the bite strength of alligators.

alligator

Then, he compared an alligator's jaws to a *Tyrannosaurus rex*'s.

He found out that *T. rex*'s bite could crush a car!

Tyrannosaurus rex
(ti-ran-uh-SAWR-uhss REKS)

Did *T. rex* roar? After studying its skull, scientists think it made a deep *whumpf, whumpf* noise!

17

Brain Size Matters

The bigger an animal's brain, the smarter it often is.

Troodon was a dog-sized dinosaur with a plum-sized brain.

Scientists think it was one of the smartest dinosaurs.

Troodon
(true-DON)

Scientists examine fossil skulls to figure out the size of dinosaur brains.

Stegosaurus was much larger—about the size of an elephant.

However, its brain was also the size of a plum.

Scientists think it wasn't very smart.

Stegosaurus
(STEG-oh-sawr-uhs)

Dinosaur Eggs

All dinosaurs hatched from eggs.

The eggs of the biggest dinosaurs were probably the size of basketballs.

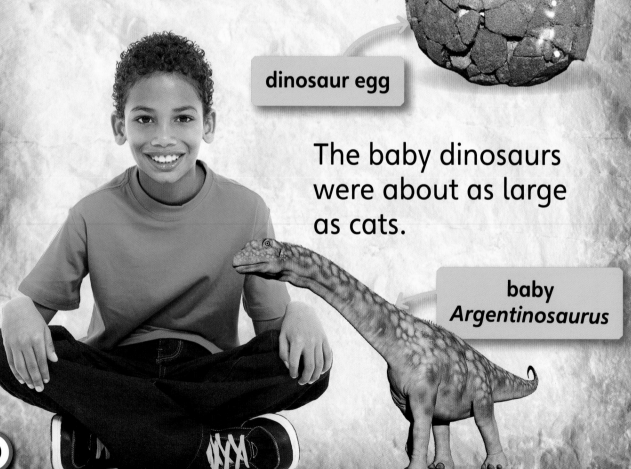

dinosaur egg

The baby dinosaurs were about as large as cats.

baby
Argentinosaurus

The bigger an egg grows, the thicker its shell gets.

Dinosaur eggs stayed pretty small so the babies inside could break through the shells!

eggshell

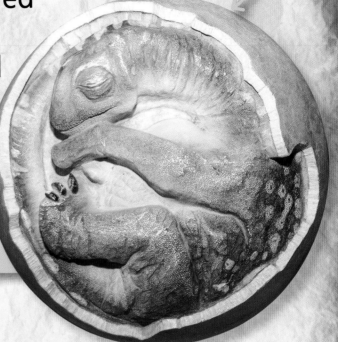

a model of a baby dinosaur inside its egg

life-size egg fossils

The tiniest dinosaur eggs found so far are less than an inch long!

Glossary

crest (KREST)
an area made of bone, feathers, or skin on an animal's head

fossils (FOSS-uhlz)
the rocky remains of animals and plants that lived millions of years ago

mate (MATE)
one of a pair
of animals that
have young
together

scientists
(SYE-uhn-tists)
people who
study nature
and the world

Index

Argentinosaurus 7, 20

claws 14–15

crests 10–11

eggs 20–21

horns 8–9

jaws 16–17

Kosmoceratops 8–9

Microraptor 7

Pachycephalosaurus 12–13

Parasaurolophus 10–11

Patagotitan 6

Stegosaurus 19

Therizinosaurus 14–15

Triceratops 8

Troodon 18

Tyrannosaurus rex 17

Read More

Halls, Kelly Milner. *Dinosaurs: Can You Tell the Facts from the Fibs? (Lie Detector).* North Mankato, MN: Picture Window Books (2015).

Wedel, Mathew J. *Totally Amazing Facts About Dinosaurs (Mind Bender).* North Mankato, MN: Capstone (2019).

Learn More Online

To learn more about dinosaurs, visit
www.bearportpublishing.com/dinosphere

About the Author

Ruth Owen has been developing and writing children's books for more than ten years. She first discovered dinosaurs when she was four years old—and loves them as much today as she did then!